The Road to Tremonte

A pilgrimage in poetry

Jakob Brønnum

ISBN: 978-81-19654-69-7

First Edition: 2024
Rs. 200/-

Cyberwit.net
HIG 45 Kaushambi Kunj, Kalindipuram
Allahabad - 211011 (U.P.) India
http://www.cyberwit.net
Tel: +(91) 9415091004
E-mail: info@cyberwit.net

Printed at Repro India Limited.

"It's never too late
but today is too soon"
Moddi

Foreword

The inspiration for this book might well be deemed presumptuous. For years, if not decades, I have sought to find the framework for a book of the kind we know from Khalil Gibran's "The Prophet" (1923) and Nietzsche's "Thus Spoke Zarathustra" (1883). I didn't seek to frame the content like Gibran and Nietzsche, with the proclaiming of various instances of truth and timeless wisdom from the wise man before his listeners and followers. I wanted to weave it into a kind of life story. Somebody suggested to me that maybe I was more inspired by Coelho's "The Alchemist" (1988), but I feel this it is not quite the case. It is said that "The Alchemist's" main theme is about finding one's destiny, though some maintain that although "The Alchemist" is as modern self-help book, woven into ancient myth and wisdom, "The Road to Tremonte", in my view, is more about trying to discover what existence as such is all about. Maybe, after all "The Road to Tremonte" has turned out a very imperfect blend of the two forms.

Sincere thanks are due to Josefine Frej Mikuta for her cover art, widening the range of the work, and for providing the motto

Jakob Brønnum, December 2023

Contents

ONE: THE BOOK OF QUESTIONS

1. What Do You Want?

I was somewhere between 14 and 17 years old
or some other age when you mix up

the color grey with the colors of the rainbow
and call it joy and call it anger

and call it confusion and call it freedom.
At that time men gathered around me

like warriors, like flies, like dogs on the leash of old age
their dark shadows clouding my vision

and they asked me, "What do you want to do with your life?"
Well, what do *you* want? I thought

what do you want to do with your life
with everybody's life, with life as such

with all the days on repeat
through all the years of idle waiting?

2. Images in the Sky

Some of them were men of my family
some of them were images in the sky

some felt it was their right to ask
expected of them by some revered tradition

some of them asked the question too early
most of them much too late

some never waited for an answer
before they began talking about themselves

or looked me in the eyes as if they had something to say
urging me to listen carefully, then telling me

what they had wanted, what they searched for,
what they lost, and what they had never found

3. The Well

I'll be honest: The question tore me apart. Something broke
deep in the mechanics of my soul

something came up and clogged my thoughts
something untouchable was disturbed.

Somewhere in the sea of emotions
a wave appeared I had tried to suppress

the wave of insecurity, doubt
and bleak expectations. What happened?

All I know is I fell into a celestial well
nobody told me even existed

my hands found nowhere to grip
the well had slippery walls or none

still, all the way down I tried to convince myself
it had to be a dream, a nightmare, an illusion

the truth is I don't know to this day if I ever
reached the bottom

4. Questions Without Answers

Other questions surrounded me like ghosts
spirits from another lifetime, popping up everywhere I went

Who am I? Where am I going? Where did I come from?
How do I get to know?

Does truth exist for life or maybe for a second only?

An ancient philosopher said: you can't get to know anything
because what you know you already know

and what you don't know you don't know how to look for
because you don't know it. I didn't believe him

or rather I didn't want to believe him

5. The Book of Questions

So, I wrote all my questions down in a notebook
that had an infinite number of pages:

Do I even exist? Am I unique? If so in relation to what?
What is needed? What is not?

When in the darkness of night everything turns around
is that a point in time or a movement in space?

Is the world a fata morgana?
Am I inside or am I outside?

The book had an infinite number of pages
so I felt I could go on and on

but before long my questions went in circles
and all possible answers were out of line

6. The Old Ghost and The Beggar

Still haunted by the oldest of the ghosts
I managed to find an answer to the original question

What do I want to do with my life?
My answer was: I want to see the world

For a moment I thought I was smart
till I saw them whispering to each other.

And when I could not stand it anymore
I snug out the door and went off on my own

I saw a poor man on the street with a sign
and a small cardboard box for coins. The sign said:

"To see the world, you have to open your eyes"
I had no coins in my pocket, as it were

when that same night I saw him in a dream,
he, on the other hand, he had no face

7. To Open Your Eyes

The sign I had seen on the street was gone
when I passed by again

the poor man was there. I wanted to ask him
if he meant open eyes or talked about something else

like an open mind, but he did not understand
focused as he was on coins. When I dreamt

about the beggar again, this time
he had a face, but his eyes were shut

and when I looked closer
I saw they were covered by coins

and as I was about to leave
I saw the face he wore was mine

8. The Dream of the Empty Notebook

I had lost my ability to pose questions
and now I tried to gaze around the corner

into the past where they all had seemed
to spring from a well of ideas. The well was gone

and when I looked into the future
I saw a bridge leading from the coast over the water

into a fog of impenetrable density.

That night I had another dream.
I found my lost book of questions

by the shore, brought in by the current
lying on an endless beach with stretches of white sand

in the dream I got so happy
like a feeling of my life having been saved

but as I picked up my trusted leatherbound book
all the pages were blank

9. Faith, Hope, and Charity

The next day I went back to the old men
and told them how they had broken my soul to pieces

with their stupid question
like when you drop a glass on the floor

not bothering to sweep up the bits
lest somebody step on them

and start leaving bloody footprints
"But you need to have faith", one of them said.

But hadn't I always had faith in myself? Except now I realized
I had opened a door to melancholy and connected with anxiety

"But you need to have hope," another of the old men said
I nodded. But what I didn't know at the time

is that when you chase your hope
sometimes you are on the escape from yourself.

"But you do need the know the meaning of charity,"
one of them said to me, and I nodded and felt I knew

except I thought he meant a charity
meant for me

10. Chasing My Illusions

For many sleepless nights and sleepy days
I pondered the questions: How does one get to know oneself?

What is there to know about life and death
if reality is a matter of scientific deduction?

Are dreams real and true or are they illusions
built by proxy for you to stay cool, calm, and collected?

On the crowded bus in the morning, I wondered:
Where do I begin and where does the other person end?

When I was walking down the street everything whispered:
When does the world begin then, and when does it end?

Is life a circle or a straight line? A birth or a death?
Will I have fallen asleep when I get to know

or will this trip evolve into an eternal nightmare?

11. Reaching the Shore

At some point you reach the shore of endless questions
pick up unsolvable problems like pebbles

start skipping stones across the water
with one question always whispering itself to you:

Will my course of life hold the truth about itself?
That's the question you cannot skip

it looks like a flat and round stone
as it lies there in the sand in front of you

you want to reach out for it
and deliver your best throw yet.

But it just won't be lifted out of its spot
no matter how hard you try

it remains too slippery, edges to sharp
and slowly but surely proves to be too heavy to move

12. The Voices and the Seagulls

And whether you are skipping stones or working hard
to understand some secret mystery of existence

or you are passing time counting the waves in the ocean
roaring towards you, not noticing the changing position

of the sun up there on the great wall of heaven
or whether you discovered you own book of symbols

in the clouds molding themselves with charms of madness
or whether you are listening to voices near you

filling up your cup, pouring water for your soul,
suddenly you look up hearing seagulls screaming

right in front of you, watching them fight for fish only they spot
under water, suddenly both time and seagulls are gone

and you're alone in the dusk, alone
with the murmur of yet another day lost in the sun

TWO: THE BOOK OF MIRRORS

13. My Secret

When I was 18 or 19, I travelled a foreign country
I had a promise to fulfill

I had been asked what I wanted to do with my life
without being able to answer

the answer I came up with - that I wanted to see the world
became a vow, a pledge, a promise.

Secretly I knew there wasn't any essence in my vow
I had made it to escape a ridiculous question

Secretly I knew why there was nothing
in the promise: How could there be if I had no direction in life

so everywhere the next unavoidable question
was posing itself to me from every corner: Who are you?

14. The Mirror

I finally discovered *who* I was:
a hazy mirror of human history

I looked at myself through images
moving faster than thoughts

little statues of clay trying in vain
to dance a cosmic dance

Occasionally I had to remind myself
that although my own life amounted to nothing

I would have to admit that life itself
is the most common and the rarest occurrence

and admit that I both knew all
there is to know about life

since it was mine from birth
and nothing at all

since everything changes
much faster than I could reflect

15. The Books I Found

I found books that said the only sane thing to do
is to commit suicide, since life is truly absurd

I found books saying the highway
leading to sanity is moving by exerting power

and book saying the only way to wisdom
is to help your neighbour and carry his burden

(I didn't have any neighbours).
I found books about how you are always

important to someone (I wasn't even important to myself)
and about how you need to make your own life matter

before you can make other's matter to you
and books about losing yourself in meditation

in stargazing, in spectral colors of the brain
fighting to gain access to yourself.

All of this was surely true
when you thought about it this way or that way

but taking it as your hope and dream
it just as soon would crumble and collapse

16. The Barren Soul

When all days were alike, and all nights were blank
I myself was that foreign country

It never occurred to me
that as much as I lived in the spur of the moment

skipping on to the next
what I was searching for

was that which makes the moment live
from the beginning onwards

and not that which fills it up in passing

17. In the Back of the Bus

Sometime later, on the way back
as life again put on its grey shades

as an invisible cloak
I was riding a bus on the highway

and the road beneath looked like
it was moving in the wrong direction.

Time seemed to have turned around down the road
and began to go backwards

I hurried to the backseat of the bus
out of the window I saw the road disappearing

moving away in constant acceleration
like a dream image of a serpent on the escape

seeking, but not finding a pit in which to hide
and wait for another chase to turn up

18. The Wall

As I recognized in front of me
the walls of my homeland rising

unconsciously trying to imagine an unknown warmth
in the colors on my day of birth

time itself had stopped and the journey I had taken
as a pledge to everyone around me

now became a mirror of empty infinity, a mirror
I lacked the courage to look in

the journey had shown itself to be a search in vain
for the spring of the well

of an unfulfilled soul
and the meaning of it all

still lost in translation

19. The Castle in the Sky

The image in the mirror I avoided chased me
it swept itself around me like a blanket

it went beaming into the hours of the day
and on into the silence of the night

forcing my gaze to go ahead of my will.
This is what the mirror showed:

The vastness of the foreign country and its open spaces
the cities of possibilities untried and unattained

the days of dizziness in trying to forget
what you ought to try to remember

all this had taken possession of my mind
fed my dreams, nourished my illusions

and built me a castle in the sky with no access
a palace of clouds encircled by a moat of air

and all I dreamt about were bridges leading nowhere

THREE: THE BOOK OF DISCOVERY

20. The End of The Road

As one day I strode around the outskirts of my city
looking for the docklands of empty emotion

trying to rediscover the place
my unsuccessful journey had ended

trying to uncover the reason I lost track in time and space
trying to connect real-time with a sea of confusion

I was trying to navigate
and maybe, just maybe find the place

in time and space where I could begin all over again

I found myself standing in the middle of nowhere
dust under my feet, electricity in the body

millions of invisible stars above
trying to rediscover a lead that was not there

21. The Naked Soul

I was more naked than a newborn baby
since the newborn does not have the capacity

to doubt life itself - that doubt you acquire
only when there have been eyes looking at

you, turning
away.

That doubt you acquire trying to fix that eye contact
only to fill your gaze with dusty wind.

That doubt you acquire when you thought
you stood up for something important

only to look around
conceding

you are all on your own

22. A Place Called Tremonte

I sat down at a local café, people talking
questioning neither themselves nor the other

In the heart of the night somebody asked me
if knew about this place called Tremonte

I had not the courage to admit I knew of no such thing
and when I tried to google

the machine was busy and politely asked me
to come back in a little while

I looked up, "What did you call it?" I asked.
But he was gone, he'd left while I had been

lost, staring deep into the wide-open spaces
of algorithm

23. The Doorman and The Prophecy

I asked around. Nobody had noticed him
and for a moment I thought he might not have been there at all

so I got up, departing out into the void of night
when at the exit I saw a cage with a parrot

at least 200 years old. I stopped to observe it
asking myself how I looked – and how old I really was

when the doorman came up to me:
"Hey you! He told me to say to you

that whatever you've been searching for
you shall find your answers there"

24. A Moment of Connection

It was like the word hit the bottom
of some hole inside of me

As if the wind itself was holding back
waiting in the shimmering light

for me to draw my breath
(I wonder who drew first)

This was a moment of connection
between feelings I had never known to be apart

25. The Advice

A voice inside began to speak
though I don't know what it had to say

and I did not recognize the tongue
I was still standing in the doorway repeating the message:

That I should visit Tremonte. Was that what he said?
But why? And where? And how?

"Did he say where it is, this place," I asked,
but the doorman was obviously busy elsewhere

and I discovered I was talking with the parrot

26. The Search

I met someone who had been around in his day -
a person clad in grey

I asked him if there was any truth
in the prophecy

I received
if there was any such place at all –

a place called Tremonte

He knew about Tremonte all right (he said)
but whether he had been he would not reveal

and when I tried to ask him for direction
I felt ashamed. I don’t know why

sometimes shame shows in the strangest
shape or form

27. The Woman by the Well

I met a young woman by the well
(could have been a dream, probably was)

drawing water for her mother
hurriedly she told me

she was not supposed to talk to strangers
but a soldier had told her about a place

he wanted to take her
when he returned from the war

he called it Tremonte or maybe Shangri-la
or maybe something else (she wasn't quite sure)

but now it was seven years since
and there had not been a word from him

so, every night she lay sleepless
wondering whether he was dead or already there

without her

28. The Glory of Tremonte

During my pursuit I met people joyously proclaiming
there was no end to the glory of Tremonte

Some held that the easy living there
and the scent of a mountain flower

known only in this region
was the reason so many sought the place

some said it was a flower as purple
as only the first light after winter solstice

some claimed breathing it just once
this scent would carry you well into a youth eternal. Look now,

I thought, is not every moment worth living potentially glorious?

If I cannot retrieve the glory of the instant
how would I be able to see the glory of Tremonte?

29. In the Eyes of Man

The glory of Tremonte, the endless glory
that's what I saw in the eyes of the man

who sat there talking to me
about it, and I believed it because I saw it.

Little did I know
about the eyes of man.

Some say the soul rests in the blood
some that the soul is a fata morgana nobody has ever seen

I believe the soul is in the eyes.
Only then I did not know

about the depths of the soul of man.

I knew about myself and my heart
I believed that if it was in there it was true

and if it was true to me
it had to be true to all. Somehow

30. The Dream About Youth

The wise man said:
When you are young

eternal youth
is such an empty promise

The wise man said:
When you grow up

you discover
you lost belief in the eternal

The wise man said:
When you grow old

you find you retain
only a dream about youth

31. The Art of Withering

When you enact the illusion
in adolescence life mimicking eternal youth

you are strangely drawn
to the art of withering -

dreaming about a civilization beyond
the apocalypse of the now

adoring ruins, being drawn
into a faltering dance of an unidentified beauty

you love simple decay, rust and dust
you adore foggy neon light and darkness

you loathe the commonness of everyday life
searching the romance of failing structures

of the past

32. The Memory

In one of these dumps, I met an old man
sitting on his own listening to the wind

he was singing a tune that reminded me
of something I knew I'd forgot

only it was the sense of having lost
I was drawn to - I had no idea

what I lost and how I had let it
slip away

33. The Old Man's Prophecy

As I passed the old man looked up
and raised his voice:

"When you see dead trees
and they look to you

like lost promises
of poetry and spirituality

when you see in petals in the rain
a memory that will be engulfed by joy when it awakes

when you see the mountain breathing
and forget about gravity

Then you will be on your way to Tremonte"

34. The Talks About the Walks

I did ask people who claimed
to have travelled there

about the road to Tremonte
I was taking part in prolonged conversations

full of mystic language
and foggy insight

about this famed walk
to a Tremonte, so very scenic:

Some said you could only reach it by foot
others talked about the need to book in advance

Some talked about the right kind of boots
some mentioned the need to bring

the water of life, hinting to me
that along the way were many deserted stretches

known to make you very lonely

35. The Most Precious Things

During this time, I wondered about the most precious things,
what they are and how to attain them

During this time, I saw that the precious things
are only precious if they come of their own accord

During this time, I learned
about the most precious things

that you can never make them come to a standstill to enjoy them
the way you cannot constrain time itself

During this time, I learned about the most precious things
that nobody touched or held them

even though they talk as if they have.
During this time, I realized that the most precious things

have never been in the market or in a bargain
never been on sale, never sold out

36. More About the Most Precious Things

I learned that whenever someone tells you about
the most precious things

claiming to know all about their origin
their shape and scope, their glittering surface

and how soft and smooth they are on the inside
if you ask them to show you or provide proof

they will tell you that though they know
them very well, in all fairness

they have to concede they heard it from somebody else
somewhere along the way

37. Endlessness and Boredom

I learned the difference
between boredom and endlessness

endlessness is to be found in words
but not in emotions

boredom is something you find in emotions
but not in deeds

endlessness can be found in deeds
but not in promises

boredom is reached in dreams
but never in seeking

not in hunger, not in yearning, not in dawning

38. Reaching the Crossroad

One Sunday walking in the rain
I felt lost and needed guidance from the breeze of passion

the road I followed led away from town
the ground grew steadily muddier, grimier, soiled

And when the night was falling from the sky
I was thirsty, maybe just a little worried, too.

There and then I came to a deserted crossroad
and had a feeling this could be the guidance I had been seeking

The crossroad truly gave no clues away.
I turned around ashamed of not possessing courage to choose

realizing my search had been driven by
simple vanity, worn out boots, and bad planning

39. The Meeting

It was then, in the dungeon of the night
I met the old woman who speaks without words

some call her The Goddess of Time
others Wisdom Eternal

I saw her face changing at every moment
yet still unchanged from the first morning

emphatically trying to convince me there is
such a thing as insight and vision

beyond word and deeds
beyond heedless striving, hollow promises

outside the glitter of artificial images of a future
that might never arrive or break out.

Wisdom is different for all her glance said,
for some it is all about heeding advice

for others it is about understanding
what is wrong with the conversation

for others yet maybe on a blessed morning
to wake up and know what the dream truly meant

FOUR: THE BOOK OF TRIADS

40. The Quest

I started a new search for the road to Tremonte. How many times now? I went to libraries and met antiquaries

I travelled the Northern hemisphere
I saw the aurora dance over the icecap

I rode through the Southern plains
where they call the wind by name

I wandered through woods so dense I did not know
whether they were made of madness or illusion

I roamed highways and byways
I saw taillights flickering into the past

41. The Truth About Tremonte

I was standing in a city made of ice
the horizon stood lined with three peaks

in a violet glint

And so finally it dawned on me that the name
Tremonte means three mountains

I closed my eyes in awe and wonder
and when I looked again, the sight was gone

but the dawn remained. And the search began anew
with a feeling that time had

caught up with itself

42. A Moment of Recognition

How do you know that what you see and feel
in your body and your mind equals a moment of understanding?

Will there be an open-ended thought
like the wind leaving the mountain coming down into the valley?

Was there a field of remembrance when everything fell in place?

Did you suddenly board a pilgrimage of your past
or was that what you just completed?

The wise man once said: “You only recognize
the moment when it’s over”

43. The Whisper of Life

It struck me now with that straightforward simplicity
I had often overlooked

if not ridiculed
that of all life's mystery and banality

can be seen in a glance
embracing these laws of threes:

There and then I convinced myself I had found the meaning
of the road to Tremonte

and I began looking for these signs
in the dome of night

in the dwindling rain
in ancient letters on white paper

known to contain a whisper of existence

44. The Triad of Thought, Will, and Emotion

Some say emotion is constituted
by thought and will

some say will is made up
of thought and emotion

some say thought is born
of emotion and will

But as I wandered the endless forests of metal debris
with naked feet and footsteps of an angel not afraid to tread

passing dogs barking, running down
the halls of museums of endless yearning

I saw the vibrant empire of the three
made up of their ever-changing relation

leading, following, mediating each other:
The triad of thought, will and emotion

45. Sensation, Duty, and Eternity

In the shade of a doubtful morning
full of loneliness and fear

there sit these men of yore
writing out their nerve-stricken pain

in the lonely flames of night
romantic melodies in their minds, hammer

on anvil, murderous thoughts
weaving threads of doomed beauty

the face of morality coldly staring
at the spirit in the wind. But it is gone

it has fallen

into the primordial chaos, dissolving
into namelessness

46. The Triad of The Process

Wait a minute, somebody said, there is nothing new
about that, everything we do is a triad

of beginning, middle and end.
Yes, I said, but how do we know where we are?

What if that which I consider to be the end of the line
shows up to be a new beginning?

And how do you explain to yourself or your companion
that even if you are on the road to Tremonte

you cannot truly know if it is still the opening
or if you are nearing the end – but is that to be understood

as if you are right in the middle of life?

47. The Triad of Skill

The philosopher said that everything you do comes in threes:
Learning, practicing, mastering

Every new morning consists of the three,
learning, practicing, mastering.

Every new meeting will require of you
that you reflect upon your response

whether you are learning, practicing
or if you profess to be mastering.

This is a truly human skill

48. The Symbol

I had struck gold
in the form of dust

Tremonte was a symbol
for progress in life

taking shape in stages of three:
seeing, walking, reaching

measuring, assessing, climbing
I decided to become a mountaineer

in the spirit of Tremonte
acknowledging that anything worth accomplishing

is found only on a pilgrimage
passing three peaks

to finally be able to be looking back
from a distance

at the turmoil of emptiness
and daily struggle

49. The Universal Spirit

It struck me that I must have
waisted a lot of possibilities

to discover something
of such a solemn and simple nature

knowing that during the search I
had collapsed and crumbled

into nothing but a name
on an empty body so far away

from any real peace of mind

50. The Fisherman and The Seventh Wave

I met a fisherman of the blue shore
he had no time for triads

“Did you not hear about
the seventh wave,”

he said. “Sit down with me and listen quietly. Count the waves.
The seventh wave has that special breath, longer and deeper

crowning the work of the others

I tell you seven is the holy number
from which you can discern

all wisdom in the world
the way you do with threes

but far above this soars the majesty of seven.

I don’t know
why it is like this

that too must be part of the wisdom”

51. The Number Twelve

I met the farmer from the ochre landscape
carrying his load on shoulders broad as the rainbow.

"There is a time for everything"
he said to me, "that is what the number twelve

will mean to you –
there is always more to do than you can finish in a day

only after twelve moons
have you reached your goal

which is no less, no more
than the blessing

of starting all over again"

52. The Temple of The Number Four

I went into the holy house where priests in red
were saying mass

One of them said: "Four is the number
of the wisdom of creation"

Another said, these are the four:
"The lion, the oxen, the eagle, and man himself"

The third priest said: "The corners of the world
and the seasons in the wind

will teach you that
the number four

does not make a square
but is a full circle"

53. The Girl and The Teacher

The girl in the garden said: "Duality
carries the holy number, everybody knows that

you and me, two is one but still the two.
This is the wisdom of love."

After this I went quiet for a day
as long as a year.

Then I heard the teacher in the school:
"Pay no attention to all that

but if you want to deal in numbers
you have to seek out truly profound numbers:

Think about pi! Think about the prime numbers
think about the cosmos of algorithm!

But be warned that numbers are empty markers only
mirrors of one-dimensional forms

for you to gather fragments of yourself
with no guarantees you ever assemble

or see the full picture."

FIVE: THE SONG OF THE MOUNTAINEER

54. The Profound

I understood there was something more profound
I had missed - I had no idea what it was

Is the knowledge that there is such a thing as the depth of life
knowledge about *something*

even as you do not have an idea what it is?
When I looked back, I saw I had been running

in all directions all the time
how would you ever find yourself

a goal in life like that?

55. The Wisdom Beyond the Peaks

There was a mountain range in that country
I visited now for the second or third time

and people there did in fact convince me that somewhere
in the blue ridges was a locality of that name

Tremonte? I repeated. They nodded
Finally, I understood: It was not the knowledge of the three

as I had thought, not only that at least,
and it was certainly not the mountain peaks themselves

which I had been searching all my life: They talked about a city
shining on a hill but still hidden - beyond these three peaks.

Maybe I had just needed to learn the lessons
before I could climb the mountain

to see the glory of Tremonte, the dream of my youth
When I passed the first mountaintop

and I saw the next in the distance, I felt
I could soon reach the goal of my life

56. The Inner Map

As I passed a man resting on a small rock
I asked for direction

He said: "Mountain paths have many twists and turns
and you cannot always be sure

what you will reach behind the next bend."
"But how do you know yourself," I asked

"I have an inner map" he said.
"I've walked back and forth here

for many years. Is it your first time here?"

57. The Last Peak

When I reached the last peak of these mountains
there still was no sense of Tremonte

and I came to wonder if I was on the right mountain
or whether Tremonte could only be accessed

from the other side
Or whether I was in the right region

or even in the right country
Or if I had misunderstood all together

the explanations I had received

As you have probably guessed
I never found it

58. The Lessons of a Weary Man

I sat down deeply disappointed with myself
I sat under a shady cliff

for seven days and seven nights
criticizing myself for not being able to understand

and for chasing mirages everywhere
and for gazing at the stars

in the heaven
when I need a footpath

and for looking for the next possible break
when in fact emptiness was all around

Then I noticed a bird singing in a distant tree.
Had it been there all along?

I don't know, at least it woke me up
and I knew I had to begin all over again

59. The Lessons of Glory

That night as I slowly woke up
with the silhouette of the bird

majestically silent
against the moon's pale face

I discovered something about glory in the eyes of man:
envy is it's fueling flame

I learned that glory exists
only if you can make other people

believe in yours and want what you have
I learned the difference

between a drop of water and the ocean
between a stone in my hand

and the mountain in the horizon
the difference between an acorn and an oak

60. The Lessons of Dreaming

I learned that every man has his own dream
I learned that because it glitters in his eyes

and because he knows for a fact that it is gold
it does not mean that it is made of gold

and even if it is gold for him, it might not be for me
the only thing it means is that he wants me

to share his dream, so he does not
have to be confined in it by himself anymore

I learned that it is not all gold that glitters

61. The First Lesson of Sharing

I learned that if somebody wants you to share his dream
and wants to tell you all about it

chances are that he has never been near it
and that he does not know where it is

because if he had it in his possession
journeying towards his own true self

he would not want anyone to know about it
lest it might break like glass wings on a butterfly

I learned that when you meet somebody
with a dream to show you

you should always ask yourself whether they are
a salesman or a saint

62. Entering the Labyrinth

So, I gave my dream up
because I understood it to be that kind of illusion

to which we commit ourselves
while waiting for reality to show up

around the corner at the end of your first youth.
I realized that this is the time

most people leave the dream behind
and begin to live a life devoid of ideals,

a life of duty and fleeting desire

This is the part of life called the beginning
of the labyrinth of endless yearning

endlessly waiting for that to show up
you never knew you were truly yearning for

63. The Promise and The Shame

Not only did you leave your dream behind
because it seemed to be the thing to do

(and everybody else were doing the same).
Not only have you been busy providing for your needs

but in that process the question you posed
which made the dream arise has slipped away

and made life a fruitless pilgrimage
towards a pit of empty space filled with useless things.

Now you do not even feel the curiosity anymore
that drove you all the way, and you do have the uncanny notion

that a promise you made yourself has been forgotten
and in the slipstream of oblivion

while shame is rolling in as a seventh wave

64. Going Downhill

Coming down the mountain
leaving endless number of peaks behind me

secretly listening for the bird
that woke me up at night

while solemnly posing with the moon

walking in the long shadows of
a life-question never answered, then ignored

I accepted that what I learned about life, I learned
trodding downhill with aching feet

65. The Urge

When I got to my home country
everything was back at the greyscale life

on the outside of the blinds
well-known voices

was going through the motions
(that's how it sounded to me)

Soon the urge was back
this time driving me away

from the spur of the moment
letting me live in the past

working the treadmill
nurturing the holes my true self

through the darkness and dust
of tumbling thoughts.

But when the spell of these long seasons
finally gave way, next year I took off again

66. The Labyrinth

When I got to that foreign country fourth time around
something had changed

but was it in my mind
or was it the world around me?

True, I did not really know the place
but still, this could be no foreign country by now

As usual, I looked in the mirror for advice
but in vain, the mirror was still empty.

Should I go home and wait for my well-known urge to travel?
Should I stay in this place and be displaced?

Life had become a labyrinth within the labyrinth
and I feared I would never live to find the way

from one labyrinth to the other

67. Where to Look for Meaning?

By now existence had fragmented itself into seconds,
places, questions, numbness, endless journeys, eyes,

flashing screens

unknown faces, empty suitcases, waiting, posing
posting, trying, walking, talking, stalking

I looked habitually around to try and catch the meaning of it all
but how to look for meaning where there is none?

What did I think would happen? That I would I find it

in the eyes of somebody I sat beside
or somebody I was talking to in the bar,

or on the beach? Everywhere I looked people's eyes
revealed short-lived dreams and drained emotion

68. Questions in a Face

I met many different people
and saw many different faces

they were all somehow
faces I recognized

yet unknown they way all faces
are different and alike.

What is in a face of a stranger?
What is in a face of a friend?

What is in the face of a lost one?
What is in the face of a newborn?

What is in the face of somebody you only met
in your dream at night and forgot again by dawn?

69. The Parable of the Dandelion

I felt I was like the dandelions in the grass:
Some of them have yet to bloom

standing there waiting
for life to happen.

Some of them are blooming
but nobody seems to take notice.

Some of them are seeding
and only children love them, everybody else

try to avoid them contaminating the lawn.
Some of them are withering away

soon to be forgotten, all of them
present at the same time in the same place

though nobody can say whether this stage or that
completes their cycle of life

70. Going in Circles

Soon I had no money
sleeping outside in the warm weather

working for the farmers getting a meal
working for the ice creams sellers getting a smile

I had come out of the labyrinth
or maybe I'd just forgotten about it

going in circles instead

71. By the Wall of Granite

One morning I was standing in front of a wall of granite
realizing it was the image of my life

At one point I put my hand in my back pocket
and felt a piece of paper

To my surprise it was my ticket home
but as I looked, it had no destination printed on it

SIX: THE WISDOM OF TREMONTE

72. The Landscape of Melancholy

Many years later I went travelling again
to see the old places and the changed faces

but the landscape itself had changed
Am I on the road to Tremonte?

I asked. The dream must have caught up with me again
without me noticing: Is that what it is all about

the dream catching up on you
revealing that if you thought otherwise

everybody notices you are clad in melancholy

73. The Man Who Walks in Darkness

I met an old man by the roadside
whom I felt I knew from somewhere

and I couldn't help asking for the road to Tremonte
like a must have done many years before

when he looked up, I realized had not met him before -

it was old age I had recognized
"The road to Tremonte," he said,

"is an expression often used in these lands
It means: You've been fooled"

74. The Same River Twice

One day in autumn I was looking at the river flowing
through the center of our town

orange foliage floating like empty boats
on the water heading towards oblivion

I was thinking about the wisdom of the philosopher
who said you can never swim in the same river twice

I still do not know exactly what he meant:

The river is the same, but the water is not
or the river is the same, but you are not?

75. Ballad of Two Seasons

I was petrified looking at
how in wintertime the water is frozen white

with black and grey and blue lines
of endless beauty

drawing memories of labyrinths and maps
of unfinished journeys

and how in the spring the water
is singing with everything coming its way

miming even the false promise
that this beauty was ever here to stay

76. The Man Passing By

I went back every morning to think
about the words of the Greek philosopher

and how he was talking to me from a place
beyond time with a voice as clear as daylight

Every day a man passed by on his bike
he was going somewhere, always in a hurry

One morning I tried to salute him
as I saw him coming up the road

he just tramped his bike a bit harder, bending forward
from a distance turning around suddenly shouting

"Get a life!"

77. Changing Darkness

If somebody calls upon you to get a life
it means that you seem like a nobody to them

(and to how many more?) though you yourself
do know you are in fact somebody

That night when I was trying to sleep in my room
darkness had changed. I felt like a stranger in my own life.

What used to be the moment of dancing thoughts
when dreams take over from consciousness and emotion

and set you free while carrying you into sleep
had now become the place of the prison of the soul

78. Staring into Faces

I needed to spend time away from the buzzle
not to see a living soul for days on end

the only face I remembered
was the face of the man on the bike

one day I understood
what I must have pondered over

for a lifetime of staring
at myself in darkened mirrors

that the more faces you meet
never truly connecting with anybody

the more common they all are

79. The Lecture

One day I was deemed so aged as to be asked
to lecture about my life and experiences

and I decided to talk about The Road to Tremonte
I talked about all my doubts

and my search
for something to search for

I talked about mornings dawning
to instantly turn into nights

leaving no traces
neither caresses nor guilt

I talked about being naked in the desert of thoughts
not knowing whether the baking sun

is the image of the holy of the holiest
or death itself. I talked about spending

your life trying to choose one or the other
not being able to make up your mind

and time was up

80. The Meaning of Tremonte

Somebody came up to me and spoke
in a voice of meekness and distress

"I'm sorry Sir, to pretend to know more than you
having given such a splendid lecture

but I am quite convinced
that you're not right about Tremonte.

The Road to Tremonte is an expression
meaning being able to live while you learn

The Road to Tremonte makes one feel alive while searching
for the meaning of it all, knowing there are no other

moments in life more precious than this,
and no later time will be ever dearer"

81. The Departure

I had been on the road all my life
searching for the road to Tremonte

only learning that the most valuable
events in life take place while we look the other way.

And then it happened again: While I looked
in the other direction as somebody

passed by to shake my hand
she disappeared before I could even ask her name

not to speak about memorizing
the lines in her face

82. The Ritual and the Urge

I wanted to travel for the last time
just to look back at things from a perspective

So, I went back out on the tracks again
on the road, and off, as usual.

The urge didn't return
only the ritual of getting to know faces

watching and discovering a searching soul
similar to the one I used to be

but I was not able to get to know anybody
my mind was filled with the urge

to remember the face of the girl
who finally directed me to the truth

about the road to Tremonte

83. The Wisdom of Tremonte

This is why I never reached Tremonte
and never knew I was always on the road to it:

As long as I travelled on my own
Tremonte would never rise before me

since whatever you see and whatever you learn
and whatever you feel and wherever you go

whatever insight you
stumble upon

or slowly attain through ordinary hard work
you can never genuinely make your own

what hasn't been shared with a living soul

Notes

4. Plato quotes Socrates expressing this view.
7. Coins upon the eyes: Meaning being ready for the boat ride on the river Styx to the underworld, according to popular, probably modern interpretation of Greek mythology.
9. Faith, hope, and charity, cf. 1 Corinthians 13.
14. Little statues of clay. The Alchemists the Homunculus. It appears to be Paracelsus (1493-1541) who first made an Homonculus
15. Life as absurd and committing suicide as the only sensible thing to do: The provocative thought in Camus' The Myth of Sisyphos (1942) - Exerting power: A main thought in the philosophy of Nietzsche - Help and carry: The New Testament principle that Nietzsche opposes in his philosophy
39. The female as the image of wisdom is found in Plato: The Symposium (ca. 370 BC), The Shepherd of Hermas (ca AD 200), Boethius: The Consolation of Philosophy (AD 524) as well as the Kabbalah and elsewhere
42. The wise man: Søren Kierkegaard (1813-55)
44. Not afraid to tread: A line in Alexander Pope's poem An Essay on Criticism (1711) reads: "For fools rush in where angels fear to tread". Quoted by Bob Dylan in Jokerman (1983) and the title of a novel by E. M. Forster (1953)
45: Sensation, Duty, and Eternity: Equivalent to Kierkegaard's three stages in life, the aesthetic, the ethical, and the religious
47: The Triad of Episteme, Techne, and Fronesis: Aristotle's interpretation of practical wisdom
52: The lion, the oxen, the eagle, and man himself: The ancient symbols of the four gospels
55: At city shining on a hill, cf. Matthew 5:14
74: The same river twice: Heraclitus (ca 500 BC)

www.ingramcontent.com/pod-product-compliance
Lightning Source LLC
Chambersburg PA
CBHW022159160726
48282CB00024B/257

9788119654697